Summary of

NEVER SPLIT THE DIFFERENCE :
Negotiating As If Your Life Depended On It

by Chris Voss and Tahl Raz
Go BOOKS

Disclaimer

Note to readers:

This is an unofficial summary and analysis of Chris Voss and Tahl Raz's book "Never Split the Difference: Negotiating As If Your Life Depended On It," designed to enrich your reading experience. Buy the original book at Amazon_Never Split the Difference: Negotiating As If Your Life Depended On It.

respective trademark holders. These trademark holders are not affiliated with us, and they do not sponsor or endorse our publications. This book is unofficial and unauthorized. It is not authorized, approved, licensed, or endorsed by the aforementioned interests or any of their licensees.

The information in this book has been provided for educational and entertainment purposes only.

The information contained in this book has been compiled from sources deemed reliable, and it is accurate to the best of the Author's knowledge; however, the Author cannot guarantee its accuracy and validity and cannot be held liable for any errors or omissions. Upon using the information contained in this book, you agree to hold harmless the author from and against any damages, costs, and expenses, including any legal fees, potentially resulting from the application of any of the information provided by this guide. The disclaimer applies to any damages or injury caused by the use and application, whether directly or indirectly, of any advice or information presented, whether for breach of contract, tort, neglect, personal injury, criminal intent, or under any other cause of action. You agree to accept all risks of using the information presented inside this book.

The fact that an individual or organization is referred to in this document as a citation or source of information does not imply that the author or publisher endorses the information that the individual or organization provided. This is an unofficial summary and analytical review and has not been approved by the original author of the book.

Table of Contents
Summary of Never Split the Difference: Negotiating As If Your Life Depended On It by Chris Voss and Tahl Raz

OVERVIEW OF NEVER SPLIT THE DIFFERENCE: NEGOTIATING AS IF YOUR LIFE DEPENDED ON IT

Negotiation is a very important skill that everyone must possess in order to deal with multiple situations, expected or unexpected. In *"Never Split the Difference,"* author Chris Voss tells us, with real-life examples, about the various aspects of and requirements for negotiating successfully.

CHAPTER 1 OF NEVER SPLIT THE DIFFERENCE: NEGOTIATING AS IF YOUR LIFE DEPENDED ON IT: THE NEW RULES

"How to Become the Smartest Person ... in Any Room" — The author starts the book with an anecdote from his life. He had more than twenty years' experience as a negotiator, including time as a lead international kidnapping negotiator of the FBI. Now he was at the Harvard Law School for a short executive negotiating course, to learn new skills from the business world's approach. He was suddenly set up to join a (mock) negotiating situation with few top professors. In the scenario, his son had been kidnapped and would be killed if $1 million was not given immediately! But by throwing many open-ended questions, the author outwitted the professors by asking repeatedly about the logistics of delivering the ransom, for which the professors were not prepared. He visited Harvard a year later for the winter negotiation course, where he again managed to beat the brightest students —by using the best tricks based on logic, value, intellectual power, and moral concepts about fairness — repeatedly in stimulated negotiation situations with his old-school, experiential knowledge.

Hostage-taking is not new; it has existed since the early times of recorded history. But in the late twentieth century, it became more frequent. The

Munich Olympics tragedy and the Attica prison riots in New York had sad endings. After a hostage-taking situation in Florida that resulted in three deaths — for which the FBI was later blamed for its poor approach — the New York City Police Department, followed by the FBI and others, put together dedicated teams of specialists to design a process to handle crisis negotiations. The Harvard Negotiation Project was founded in 1979 with a mandate to improve the theory, teaching, and practice of negotiation, and in 1981, two of its co-founders published a new thesis , "Getting to Yes," that brought a sea change. It had four primary tenets: separate the person from the problem; don't get wrapped up in the other side's position but focus on their interests; work together to create win-win options; and establish mutually agreed-upon standards for evaluating the possible solutions. In Chicago, professors Tversky and Kahneman brought out a theory showing that man is a very irrational beast and all humans suffer from cognitive bias. They outlined about 150 irrational brain processes, including: (a) the Framing Effect, which proves people respond differently to the same choice depending on how it is framed, (b) the Prospect Theory, which explains why we take unwarranted risks in the face of uncertain losses, and (c) the concept of Loss Aversion, which shows that people are statistically more inclined to avoid a loss than to achieve an equal gain. These were all codified in Kahneman's 2011 bestseller, "Thinking, Fast and Slow." Man, he wrote, has two systems of thought: System 1, our animal mind, is fast, instinctive, and emotional, while System 2 is slow, deliberative, and logical. System 1 guides and steers our rational thoughts.

A few later kidnapping negotiations proved that the theory of "Getting to Yes" was not working in real situations. In classic bargaining situations, the problem-solving approach was not the best technique. Most of the real situations were emotionally driven, and to handle them, negotiation skills must focus on the irrational and the emotional. The requirements were simple psychological tactics and strategies to calm people down, establish trust and rapport, and encourage verbalization and empathy. The concept of Tactical Empathy is the centerpiece of this book.

We must be able to negotiate well in various situations in life to get the best for ourselves, and this book guides us to achieve that.

CHAPTER 2 OF NEVER SPLIT THE DIFFERENCE: NEGOTIATING AS IF YOUR LIFE DEPENDED ON IT: BE A MIRROR

"How to Quickly Establish Rapport"— This chapter teaches us how to avoid the assumptions that confuse new negotiators and replace them with techniques like Mirroring, Silences, and the Late-Night FM DJ Voice.

In September 1993, masked bank robbers entered a Chase Manhattan Bank branch in Brooklyn. They injured the guard and a teller and locked them up. When the FBI was notified about the hostage-taking, the author, who was then part of the FBI's Joint Terrorism Task Force, and a colleague reached the site, which was already swarmed by other agencies like NYPD and SWAT. The different teams had set up shop in different locations around the bank with various vantages.

Negotiations had to be done with the robbers to ensure the safe release of the hostages. The author speaks about the importance of the negotiators' use of their skills to reveal the surprises that would exist. Negotiation should be approached with a mindset of discovery, and the goal should be to extract as much information as possible. In this hostage crisis, the initial expectation was that it would end quickly and that the robbers wanted to surrender. The lead robber was sending false messages and misleading the negotiators with the intent to confuse them. He spoke about his team and their instructions, but in reality, by the time the police had reached the place, three of the robbers including the driver of the getaway vehicle had already bolted, and only two were left in the bank holding the hostages. One of these two robbers was the leader and the other a reluctant partner. But all these details emerged much later.

The FBI team's Negotiation Operation Center (NOC) was set up very close to the bank, which put them at a disadvantage, as there was no buffer. The author was assigned to coach Joe, the police negotiator. There were others around them to listen to the conversations with the robbers and gauge the mood. The goal was to identify the exact requirements of their counterparts and make them feel safe and talk more. The lead robber kept asking for an escape van so that he, along with his fellow robbers, could escape with the hostages. He was keen to give the impression that the hostages were being well taken care of. Joe was doing a good job talking with him. Simultaneously, the other investigators checked all the cars in the area and established and spoke to all their owner except one, which they rightly assumed belonged to Chris Watts, one of the robbers. At this point, the author took over the talking part from Joe and started speaking to the lead robber in a genial tone, which he calls the FM DJ tone, to soothe flared nerves and cool the situation. He asked to speak to one of the hostages, and a lady said only, "I am okay," before being cut off. By using the technique called Mirroring, the author repeated the queries of the robber and extracted more details about the getaway car and the driver. The author then asked the lead robber whether he was Chris Watts, and he naturally said no. At this point, another robber took over the conversation, and he was less tough. The author took command and told him, "Nobody gonna get hurt," and he sounded relieved. This guy was ready to escape, as he had been reluctant in the first place. The negotiating team managed to get him to escape and surrender. Another seasoned negotiator, Dominick, took over for the author to speak to the lead robber. He got the hostages to walk out one by one, and finally Chris Watts also walked out and was arrested.

The author, in his book, speaks about a few steps during these negotiation talks: use the late-night FM DJ voice; start with "I'm sorry …"; mirror; silence for at least four seconds to let the mirror work its magic on your counterpart; AND repeat. We must: slow things down and make the counterparty feel safe enough to reveal themselves; discern between wants (aspirations) and needs (the bare minimum for a deal); and laser-focus on what the other party has to say.

CHAPTER 3 OF NEVER SPLIT THE DIFFERENCE: NEGOTIATING AS IF YOUR LIFE DEPENDED ON IT: DON'T FEEL THEIR PAIN, LABEL IT

"How to Create Trust with Tactical Empathy"— Here we delve into Tactical Empathy and learn how to recognize our counterpart's perspective and then gain trust. We also learn about understanding through labeling, how to defuse negative dynamics, and how to disarm our counterpart's complaints using the "accusation audit."

The year was 1998, and the author was in New York amid another difficult situation. Three heavily armed fugitives were holed up in an apartment after a firefight with another gang. The author was the primary negotiator. There were snipers from his team in adjacent buildings ready to strike. In this incident, there was no telephone to contact the people inside the apartment, so the author and his team had to speak through the apartment doors for more than six hours. With his late-night FM DJ voice, the author finally convinced the people inside, first a lady then three fugitives, to come out. During the debriefing, they gave the reason why they decided to give in: "We did not want to get caught or get shot, but you calmed us down…We finally believed you…"

The concept of Tactical Empathy had been applied here. It is about understanding the feelings and mindset of the other at the moment and hearing what is behind those feelings, so you increase your influence in all the moments that follow. Attention is drawn to both the emotional obstacles and potential pathways to reach an agreement. Even expert negotiators good at this technique find articulating their methods difficult.

The next technique discussed is labeling. It is about identifying the feelings of their counterparts, turning them into words, and calmly repeating their emotions back to them. This shows that we are acknowledging their emotions and saves time in developing confidence during the negotiations. It helps defuse negative emotions and pick up tiny clues of information. Labels mostly should begin with almost the same words: "It seems like…", "It sounds like…", "It looks like…", though the end result will differ as per the situation. The final rule in labeling is silence. Once we throw out a label, we should be quiet and listen and give the other party time to respond without jumping in to speak further.

How we use labeling goes a long way in determining the success of the entire negotiation. The author quotes the example of a grumbly grandpa during a family reunion. He acts cranky, and with the right labeling technique, like "we don't see each other," we can bring out the real cause behind his behavior which might be that he is not being visited frequently or he is feeling neglected. People's emotions generally have two layers; one is shown on the external side, and the other is internal — the second one is the key to understanding the state of mind and then offering a solution. In the grandpa's case, it can be an assurance that he will be visited more often and spoken to more frequently.

Defusing negative dynamics helps a lot, especially when the mistake is from our side. Acknowledging it and facing the situation headlong with an apology or with action in an open manner will defuse the hurt feelings and calm the other side. Negativity is a difficult feeling, and the best way to deal with negativity is to observe it without reaction and without judgment. Then, we must consciously label each negative feeling and replace it with positive, compassionate, and solution-based thoughts.

The accusation audit technique, when done in advance, helps prepare oneself in the negotiation to head off negative dynamics before they take root. Imagining all the terrible things that the counterparty could say to us is called the accusation audit. This helps in preparing for difficult situations and being ready to tackle them during negotiations. By using this technique, we can acknowledge the counterpart's biggest gripes, and because this calms the other party, who feels that we are able to see their version of things, negotiations become easier.

CHAPTER 4 OF NEVER SPLIT THE DIFFERENCE: NEGOTIATING AS IF YOUR LIFE DEPENDED ON IT: BEWARE "YES"—MASTER "NO"

"How to Generate Momentum and Make It Safe to Reveal the Real Stakes" —For good negotiators, the word "No" is pure gold, while "Yes" and "Maybe" are often worthless. The author narrates how he joined the FBI Joint Terrorism Task Force (JTTF) in New York after being transferred from Pittsburgh following a two-year stint. He wanted desperately to join the JTTF, though he was not qualified to join it. He met with Amy Bonderow, who ran the FBI Crisis Negotiation team. Despite her attempts to shoo him away for his "No" answers to all her questions, when she asked him about his credentials and relevant experience, he persisted with his request to join and said there should be something that he could do. She laughed and asked him to volunteer at the suicide hotline but made no guarantees of him later joining the JTTF. He discovered that saying "No" and receiving "No" answers could sometimes act as a gateway to resolution in a negotiation. A "No" could mean many things like:

I am not yet ready to agree;

You are making me feel uncomfortable;

I do not understand;

I don't think I can afford it;

I need more information;

I want to talk it over with someone else.

Follow these conversations by asking solution-based questions or simply labeling their effect: "What about this doesn't work for you?" "What would you need to make it work?" "It seems like there's something here that bothers you." By doing this, we can move closer to resolution.

There are three kinds of "Yes" — Counterfeit (when the counterparty plans to say No but says Yes to keep the conversation going until he finds another route), Confirmation (a reflexive answer to a black-and-white question and generally innocent), and Commitment (which is the real deal and what is required from the negotiation). Identifying and getting the commitment "Yes" and affirming it a few times is the key.

The author began volunteering with the Suicide Helpline, and after a period, he had his performance review done by Jim, who sat and listened to a phone conversation that the author was having with one of the regular callers as part of the review. The author felt he had done well, but the supervisor, a seasoned veteran, called it one of the worse calls he had heard and explained why. Daryl, the counterparty in the call, had congratulated the author for having done a good job, but the supervisor identified that it was more to get off the call for the moment and continue another day. Using rapport and getting connection and agreement is useful, but unless we can get the counterparty to totally commit and agree, the discussion is a failure. The author took the time to digest this fact. Having learned this lesson, the author applied the new learnings in his next calls, and when he met with Amy after five months, she was happy with his work and gave him the position he had coveted.

A "No" answer protects people from making ineffective decisions and slows the conversation down to let people revisit and freely embrace things and make them feel secure. This moves all efforts forward. By swapping "Yes" for "No" answers in conversations and altering the discussion, we can get into the driver's seat and be in charge.

Even in email conversations, when the other party plays tough or ignores emails, provoking a "No" from them can help to resume communication. For example, by emailing the other party something like, "Have you given up on this project?" he is forced to say "No" and resume discussions.

CHAPTER 5 OF NEVER SPLIT THE DIFFERENCE: NEGOTIATING AS IF YOUR LIFE DEPENDED ON IT: TRIGGER THE TWO WORDS THAT IMMEDIATELY TRANSFORM ANY NEGOTIATION

" How to Gain the Permission to Persuade" —This chapter examines ways to make the counterparty feel understood and positively affirmed in a negotiation and why we should strive for "That's right" instead of "Yes" at every stage of a negotiation, as well how to use summaries and paraphrasing in negotiations.

In August 2009, the militant group Abu Sayyaf in the Philippines captured a CIA agent, Jeffrey Schilling, and a ransom of $10 million was asked for his release. As part of the Crisis Negotiation Unit (CNU) of the FBI, the author was involved in the negotiations. The CNU had developed the Behavioral Change Stairway Model (BCSM) that proposed five stages — active listening, empathy, rapport, influence, and behavioral change — in negotiation processes. When someone is taken up the five-stage stairway of this model, at some point there will be a breakthrough moment.

The author, along with his partner, was running the negotiation process and traveling to Manila frequently to guide and strategize. Abu Sabaya was the key negotiator from Abu Sayyaf and was a veteran rebel with a violent past. He had arrived at the figure of $10 million based on a few other payments that had been made in similar situations elsewhere. The discussion took months, and as Abu Sayyaf was trying to establish an Islamic state and fighting with the government, he wanted to call the ransom money war damages. Benjie, a Filipino military officer and an honest patriot, was involved in the negotiations guided by the author. He hated Abu Sabaya for his misdeeds and was therefore not in the right frame of mind to employ the steps enumerated by the author. The author's first task was to bring him out of his mindset through open discussions and negotiation. He had to engage him in a conversation that led him to say, "That's right." Once done, Benji was driving the negotiations with Abu Sabaya to get a "That's right" from him. He was coached with a two-page manual that told him to employ the following in his discussions: effective pauses, minimal encouragers, mirroring, labeling, and paraphrase and summarize.

When Abu Sabaya called Benjie next time, Benjie followed the script, and when he finally paraphrased and summarized, Abu Sabaya could not help saying, "That's right." The demand for war damages disappeared. His interest in holding the hostage diminished, and the hostage was able to escape due to reduced vigilance. He later told Benjie that his final conversation kept him from harming the hostage.

Getting a "That's right" is a great winning strategy. It should not be confused with the statement "You're right." When someone says, "You're right," it is more likely that it is said just to keep the other person away for a while, not because the person actually agrees. The efforts should be focused on getting the "That's right" affirmation. It helps in many situations like when making a sale or in one's career, such as a job change or a promotion. Getting the other party to say, "That's right," means the negotiation is successfully complete.

CHAPTER 6 OF NEVER SPLIT THE DIFFERENCE: NEGOTIATING AS IF YOUR LIFE DEPENDED ON IT: BEND THEIR REALITY

"How to Shape What Is Fair" — This chapter helps discover the art of "bending reality," that is, employing a variety of tools for framing a negotiation in such a way that the counterparty unconsciously accepts the limits we place on the discussion. We learn how to navigate deadlines to create urgency and how to employ the idea of fairness to nudge the counterparty and make them feel that not accepting our offer would be a loss.

In 2004, in Haiti's capital, Port-au-Prince, a leading politician's aunt was kidnapped, and the ransom demand was $150,000 to be paid immediately, or she would be killed. Haiti was going through troubled times then, and kidnappings for ransom were common. The politician was worried, and the FBI was requested to help. As per conventional negotiating logic, offering the kidnappers $75,000 would seem reasonable, as it would appear win-win, but this satisfies neither side. Compromise means "splitting the difference" and is often a bad deal.

The key theme here is that "no deal" is better than a bad deal. It is like a man wearing a black shoe and a brown shoe as a compromise when the husband wanted to wear black shoes and the wife wanted him to wear brown shoes. The author says here that the simple rule is: *"Never Split the Difference."* In negotiation, time plays an important role, and a looming deadline creates panic. In reality, at least in the private sector, where working to meet deadlines is a way of life, missing deadlines has seldom led to disaster. Deadlines are often flexible and arbitrary.

In the Haiti case, it was noticed that Monday was a busy day when the thugs would engage in a lot of talks because they wanted to get paid as the weekend approached. Slowly, the realization dawned that they were after some money to have a nice weekend, and $150,000 was too high and a lot less would suffice. The good negotiators started paying attention to how many of the questions that identified What, Who, When and How were addressed. Even car dealers and salespeople work doubly hard during month-ends and quarter-ends to meet targets and are most vulnerable to closing a deal during those times. Deadlines cut both ways. When negotiation is over for one side, it is over for the other side, too. So deadlines are not something to be hidden, as they increase impasse. Rather, if we tell the counterparties about the deadlines, chances are that we get better deals. More than deadlines, it is more important to engage in the process to get to know how long it will take.

While we may use logic to reason ourselves to a decision, the actual decision-making is governed by emotions. The most powerful word in negotiations is "Fair," and knowing when and how to use it holds the key to resolving crisis situations. People go to all extents to resist what they perceive as "Unfair;" for example, Iran is suffering from sanctions due to its perception that the restrictions on its nuclear problem are unfair, but the country is still holding out. In situations like the sale of a home or a fight for a better pay deal with the NFL Players Association— the usage of the word "fair" at the right moment defuses difficult situations. In negotiation situations, the author uses it early by saying, "I want you to feel that you are being treated fairly at all times…" This sets him up early as an honest dealer and builds a reputation for being fair.

Knowing the emotional drivers of the counterparties helps in a big way. While our decisions may be irrational, there are still consistent patterns, principles, and rules behind how we act. By knowing them, we can plan to influence them. This leads to the Prospect Theory discussed earlier and the tendency of people towards Loss Aversion. To get real leverage, we must persuade the other side that they would lose something concrete if the deal fell through. In discussions, the following help: (a) anchor the counterparty's emotions, (b) let the other party go first most of the time to know their views, (c) establish a range, say between $ 35,000 and $ 38,500 in a discussion on expected salary, keeping our required level at the lower end of the band (here $35,000), (d) pivot to mon-monetary terms that are easier for the counterparty to give, like perks, (e) use odd numbers when talking in numbers and using less rounded figures like $37,263 and (f) surprise with a gift.

Going back to the Haiti deal, when it became certain that the kidnappers wanted money just for partying, the family was ready to pay $50,000 to $85,000. But the author decided to bring it down further to $5,000.

After discussing and haggling using the "range" and "odd numbers" techniques, the deal was finalized by a payment of $4,751 and a CD stereo set, and the aunt was freed!

CHAPTER 7 OF NEVER SPLIT THE DIFFERENCE: NEGOTIATING AS IF YOUR LIFE DEPENDED ON IT: CREATE THE ILLUSION OF CONTROL

"How to Calibrate Questions to Transform Conflict into Collaboration" —This chapter is about the incredibly powerful tool "calibrated questions," which is comprised of the queries that begin with "How?" or "What?" and how they force our counterparty to apply their mental energy to solving our problems. In May 2001, the Abu Sayyaf group(the same group discussed in an earlier chapter) raided a diving resort in the Philippines and took twenty hostages including three Americans. Two among the Americans were a missionary couple, while the third, Sobero, ran a California waterproofing firm. This kidnapping and rescue effort went wrong right from the beginning. Immediately after the kidnapping, the Philippines president declared an all-out war against the Abu Sayyaf group. As American hostages were involved, the FBI and CIA were called in. Several raids happened but resulted only in several hostages getting raped and killed. The crisis ended in June 2002 amid gunshots, and the author regards this as the biggest failure in his entire career. The lessons that the FBI learned from this event were that negotiation was coaxing and not overcoming, co-opting and not

defeating. Successful negotiation involves giving the counterparty the illusion of control while getting him to do what we want him to do.

When the author got involved in this crisis, the Philippines military was bombing the hospital in which the kidnappers and hostages were holed up. By the next morning, the kidnappers had moved out with the hostages, and it was later discovered they used leaked information of army movements from someone inside the army. During negotiations, the Americans were kept away from the calls with convenient excuses. Further parallel discussions were going on with a member of a cabinet, and the hostage-takers promised not to kill anyone. Something went wrong, and Sobero was beheaded. During this time, 9/11 happened, the Abu Sayyaf group was linked to Al Qaeda, and US interest in this episode suddenly shot up. The author was again sent to negotiate. At this point, someone else released $300,000 from a donor to the kidnappers. The money vanished, but no one was set free. It was totally a muddled atmosphere. When they got wind that the kidnappers were in a forest, the Philippine Scout Rangers surrounded the area and opened fire, indiscriminately raining bullets. The husband from the American couple died while the wife survived with injuries. There were several failures and loose points in this entire sag — parallel negotiations, underground dealings, mistrust, political maneuvering, intelligence failure, betrayal, and lack of communication.

Giving the counterparty the illusion of control by asking calibrated questions — by asking for help — is a powerful tool. By asking these questions, the listener is given a sense of importance, and the feeling that he is being heard gives him an illusion of control — and the party asking the questions then can act appropriately to get the required concessions. "He who has learned to disagree without being disagreeable has discovered the most valuable secret of negotiation."

The essentials of calibrated questions:

Avoid verbs or words like, *can, is, are, do* or *does*, which make closed-ended questions that can be answered with *yes* or *no*. Instead, start with *Who, What, When, Why, Where,* and *How*. These inspire counterparties to think and reply. Of these, *What, How,* and sometimes *Why* are the best. Nothing else. The others like *Who, When,* and *Where* will only get the counterparty to share a fact, while a Why can sometimes backfire.

Depending on the situation, to get the best results in negotiations, the author recommends the use of questions like:

What about this is important to you?

How can I help to make this better for us?

How would you like me to proceed?

What is it that brought us into this situation?

How can we solve this problem?

What's the objective? / What are we trying to accomplish here?

How am I supposed to do that?

During negotiations, cultivating the habit of biting the tongue helps us slow down our impulse to reply quickly and gives us time to think and answer. Also, we should always keep in mind that in many situations, besides the individual or team we are interacting with, there may be others who matter in decision-making. We should be well acquainted with them first so that the agreements reached during discussions are not later canceled if they are not happy.

CHAPTER 8 OF NEVER SPLIT THE DIFFERENCE: NEGOTIATING AS IF YOUR LIFE DEPENDED ON IT: GUARANTEE EXECUTION

"How to Spot the Liars and Ensure Follow-Through from Everyone Else" — This chapter demonstrates how to employ these calibrated questions to guard against failures in the implementation phase. "Yes" is nothing without "How?" We discover the importance of nonverbal communication and how to use "How" questions to gently say "No."We also learn how to influence the deal-killers when they're not at the table.

The author explains that the job of a negotiator isn't just to get to an agreement.

It's getting to one that can be implemented and making sure that happens. Negotiators must be decision architects. They need to design the verbal and nonverbal elements of the negotiation to gain both consent and execution.

The author describes the case of an American who had been kidnapped in the Ecuadoran jungle by a Colombia-based rebel group. Jose and his wife, Julie, had been guiding tour groups through the jungle near the Colombian border.

The captors kidnapped Jose and demanded a sum of $5 million from Julie. The author this time wanted to try his new strategy, and that was, "All we're going to say is, 'Hey, how do we know Jose is okay? How are we supposed to pay until we know Jose is okay?' again, and again." The negotiators coached Julie every day as they waited for contact from the rebels. Julie was told to answer every one of the kidnappers' demands with a question. The strategy was to keep the kidnappers engaged but off-balance. By now, the captors had driven down the ransom to $16,500. The negotiators were happy, as the ransom was now affordable by the family, and success was within reach. And then the author got a call that Jose had escaped and was on the way home.

Due to all the delays and questions, some of the guerrillas peeled off and didn't return. "How" questions are a surefire way to keep negations going. They put pressure on your counterparty to come up with answers and to contemplate your problems with their demands.

A repetitive series of "What" and "How" questions can help us overcome the aggressive tactics of a manipulative adversary.

The 7-38-55 Percent Rule:

The author describes the rule created by ULC psychology professor Albert Mehrabian. This rule states that only 7 percent of a message is based on the words, while 38 percent comes from the tone of the voice and 55 percent from the speaker's body language and face. Body language and tone of voice — not words — are the most powerful assessment tools.

The Rule of Three:

The Rule of Three is simply getting the other guy to agree to the same thing three times in the same conversation. It's tripling the strength of whatever dynamic we're trying to drill into at the moment.

In a study of the components of lying, it has been found that liars use more words than truth-tellers and use far more third-person pronouns. They start talking about *him, her, it, one, they,* and *their* rather than *I* in order to put some distance between themselves and the lie.

The author advises saying our name in a funny, friendly way when we introduce ourselves to others. Humor and humanity are the best ways to break the ice and remove roadblocks.

CHAPTER 9 OF NEVER SPLIT THE DIFFERENCE: NEGOTIATING AS IF YOUR LIFE DEPENDED ON IT: BARGAIN HARD

"How to Get Your Price" — In this chapter, the author offers a step-by-step process for effective bargaining, including how to prepare, how to dodge an aggressive counterparty, and how to go on the offensive. We also learn the Ackerman system, the most effective process the FBI has for setting and making offers.

The author begins by explaining in detail how he was able to bargain and buy a red Toyota 4Runner. The vehicle was priced at $36,000. The author, through his negotiations, bought the vehicle for $30,000.

The author goes on to say that most negotiations hit an inevitable point where the slightly loose and informal interplay between two people turns to confrontation and the proverbial "brass tacks." You know the moment: you've mirrored and labeled your way to a degree of rapport. No part of a negotiation induces more anxiety and unfocused aggression than bargaining, which is why it's the part that is more often fumbled and mishandled than any other. Even when we have the best-laid plans, a lot of us wimp out when we get to the moment of exchanging prices.

The author explains that bargaining is not rocket science, but it's not simple intuition or mathematics, either. To bargain well, we need to shed our assumptions about the haggling process and learn to recognize the subtle psychological strategies that play vital roles at the bargaining table. Our personal negotiation style — and that of our counterparty— is formed through childhood, schooling, family, culture, and a million other factors; by recognizing it, we can identify our negotiating strengths and weaknesses and adjust our mindset and strategies accordingly.

Over the last few years in an effort primarily led by his son, Brandon, the author consolidated and simplified all the research, cross-referencing it with their experiences in the field and the case studies of their business school students, and found that people fall into three broad categories.

Some people are accommodators; some are assertives, like the author; and the rest are data-loving analysts.

Analysts:

Analysts are methodical and diligent. They are in no big rush. Instead, they believe that if they are working toward the best result in a thorough and systematic way, time is of little consequence. Their motto: As much time as it takes to get it right. They pride themselves on not missing any detail in their extensive preparation. Apologies have little value to them since they see the negotiation and their relationship with you as a person largely as separate things.

Accommodators:

The most important thing to this type of negotiator is the time spent building the relationship. Accommodators think if there is a free-flowing, continuous exchange of information, time is being well spent. They are happy as long as they are communicating. Their goal is to be on great terms with their counterparty.

Of the three types, they are most likely to build a great rapport without accomplishing anything.

Assertives:

The assertive believes that time is money and every wasted minute is a wasted dollar.

Their self-image is linked to how much they can get accomplished in a period of time. Assertives love winning above all else, often at the expense of others. Most of all, assertives want to be heard. They focus on their own goals rather than people.

The author describes how negation academics like to operate with excessively rational processes devoid of emotion. They talk about the ZOPA — Zone of Possible Agreement — which is where the seller's and buyer's zones cross. Say Tony wants to sell his car and won't take less than $5,000, and Samantha wants to buy but won't pay more than $6,000. The ZOPA runs from$5,000 to $6,000. Some deals have a ZOPA, and some don't.

The Ackerman Model: This model is an offer/counter-offer method and an effective system for beating the usual lackluster barraging dynamic. The systematic and easy-to-remember process has only six steps:

1. Set your target price.

2. Set your first offer at 65 percent of your target price.

3. Calculate three raises of decreasing increments: to 85,95, and 100 percent.

4. Use a lot of empathy and different ways to say "No."

5. When calculating the final amount, use non-round numbers like $37,893 rather than $38,000.

6. On the final number, throw in a non-monetary item to show that you're at your limit.

The author says that the genius of this system is that it incorporates the psychological tactics — reciprocity, extreme anchors, loss aversion, and so on — without us needing to think about them.

The author then goes on to explain in detail about his student Mishary, who signed a rental contract for $1,850/month. But the landlord wanted to re-up the rent at $2,100/month for ten months or $2,000/month for a year. Mishary requested a sit-down with his rental agent. He did research on the buildings around the neighborhood and how they were offering much lower prices. After a lot of negotiations and following the Ackerman model, Mishary was able to rent the house for $1,829/month.

CHAPTER 10 OF NEVER SPLIT THE DIFFERENCE: NEGOTIATING AS IF YOUR LIFE DEPENDED ON IT: FIND THE BLACK SWAN

"How to Create Breakthroughs by Revealing the Unknown Unknowns" —This chapter explains how to find and use those rarest of negotiation animals: the Black Swan. In every negotiation, there are between three and five pieces of information that, were they to be uncovered, would change everything. The concept is an absolute game-changer. We learn how to recognize the markers that show the Black Swan's hidden nest, as well as simple tools for employing Black Swans to gain leverage over our counterparty and achieve truly amazing deals.

In June 1981, there was a hostage crisis in Rochester, New York, when William Griffin shot and killed his mother and a wallpaper man, as well as injuring his stepfather, at home without warning. He then jogged to a bank two blocks away and took hostage nine employees and ordered the customers to leave. For the next three and a half hours, there was a violent stand-off with the police, who were alerted by a silent alarm. He shot many passers-by in addition to policemen and fired more than 100 rounds. He led the nine employees into a room and asked the manager to call the police and tell them to come to the entrance doors and have a shootout with him at 3 p.m. She made the call, and at 3 p.m. he dragged a teller to the main door and shot her in full view of the police. He was killed by a sniper.

The theory of Black Swan tells us that things happen that were previously thought to be impossible or never thought of at all. Risk analyst Nassim Nicholas Taleb popularized it with his books, but the term is much older. Events like Pearl Harbor, 9/11, recent banking crises, and the Internet are some examples of Black Swans. None of these were predicted, but they had far-reaching consequences. During negotiations, there are *known knowns*, *known unknowns*, and *unknown unknowns*. The third ones are Black Swans.

In the hostage event discussed above, there were several unrelated blind clues and events that were not captured and related in time. In general, hostage-takers want to be heard, respected, and spoken to. In this case, the guy did not. While the bank holdup was happening, news came in that there had been a double homicide in a house nearby, but the police did not connect these two events. When bits and pieces of a case don't add up, it's usually because our frames of reference are off; unless we break free of our expectations, they will never add up.

What we don't know can kill us or our deals. Finding the Black Swans—those powerful unknown unknowns—is intrinsically difficult, however, because we don't know the questions to ask.

Below are some of the best techniques for flushing out the Black Swans—and exploiting them:

Remember, your counterparty might not even know how important the information is or that they shouldn't reveal it. So keep pushing, probing, and gathering information.

Let what you know—our known knowns—guide you but not blind you. Every case is new, so remain flexible and adaptable.

Black Swans are leverage multipliers. There are three types of leverage: positive (the ability to give someone what they want); negative (the ability to hurt someone); and normative (using your counterparty's norms to bring them around).

Work to understand the other side's "religion." Digging into worldviews inherently implies moving beyond the negotiating table and into the life, emotional and otherwise, of your counterparty.

Review everything you hear from your counterparty. You will not hear everything the first time, so double-check. Compare notes with team members. Using backup listeners whose job is to listen between the lines is always helpful. They will hear things you miss.

Exploit the similarity principle. People are more apt to concede to someone they share a cultural similarity with, so dig for what makes them tick and show that you share common ground with them.

When someone seems irrational or crazy, they most likely aren't. Some of the mistakes that lead to crazy behavior of the counterparts are when (a) they are ill-informed, (b) they are constrained, and (c) they have other interests. Faced with this situation, search for constraints, hidden desires, and bad information.

You should try to get face time with the counterpart. Ten minutes of face time often reveals more than days of research. Pay special attention to the counterpart's verbal and nonverbal communication at unguarded moments—at the beginning and the end of the session or when someone says something out of line.

BACKGROUND INFORMATION OF NEVER SPLIT THE DIFFERENCE: NEGOTIATING AS IF YOUR LIFE DEPENDED ON IT

"Never Split the Difference: Negotiating As If Your Life Depended On It" by Chris Voss and Tahl Raz. Good negotiation skills can make the difference between life and death, a promotion at a job or the possibility of being retrenched or passed over, a good or mediocre pay hike, and so on. In "Never Split the Difference," author Chris Voss (with Tahl Raz) tells us about his journey from being a key negotiator with the FBI and dealing with many situations involving hostage-takers and kidnappings to his current life as the head of the Black Swan Group, teaching negotiation skills to many clients.

Never Split the Difference takes us inside the world of high-stakes negotiations, revealing the skills that helped Voss and his colleagues succeed when it mattered most. He shares the nine effective principles—counterintuitive tactics we can use to become more persuasive in both our professional and personal life. Life is a series of negotiations we should be prepared for. This book takes emotional intelligence and intuition to the next level and gives the reader a competitive edge in any discussion.

BACKGROUND INFORMATION ABOUT CHRIS VOSS AND TAHL RAZ OF NEVER SPLIT THE DIFFERENCE: NEGOTIATING AS IF YOUR LIFE DEPENDED ON IT

CHRIS VOSS is one of the preeminent practitioners and professors of negotiating skills in the world. He is the founder and principal of the Black Swan Group, a consulting firm that provides training and advises Fortune 500 companies through complex negotiations. Voss has taught for many business schools, including the University of Southern California's Marshall School of Business, Georgetown University's McDonough School of Business, Harvard University, MIT's Sloan School of Management, and Northwestern University's Kellogg School of Management, among others.

TAHL RAZ uncovers big ideas and great stories that ignite change and growth in people and organizations. He is an award-winning journalist and co-author of the New York Times bestseller "Never Eat Alone." He coaches executives, lectures widely on the forces transforming the new world of work, and serves as an editorial consultant for several national firms.

AWARDS AND ACCOLADES

Chris Voss

• Founder and principal of the Black Swan Group
• Advises Fortune 500 companies and taught for many business schools

Tahl Raz
• Award-winning journalist and coauthor of the New York Times bestseller "Never Eat Alone."

COVER QUESTIONS OF NEVER SPLIT THE DIFFERENCE: NEGOTIATING AS IF YOUR LIFE DEPENDED ON IT

1. What is the main idea of "Never Split the Difference"?

2. How did the author's experience in the FBI help in his later career?

3. What are Black Swans?

4. Discuss known knowns, known unknowns, and unknown unknowns?

5. Why is listening important during negotiations?

6. How is "that's right" different from "you're right"?

7. How did the author de-escalate a crisis using the late-night FM DJ voice?

8. What are the negotiation skills required to succeed in the workplace?

9. How does following the Ackerman model help during negotiations?

10. How can we make people respond to our emails when they refuse to reply?

TRIVIA QUESTIONS ABOUT NEVER SPLIT THE DIFFERENCE: NEGOTIATING AS IF YOUR LIFE DEPENDED ON IT

1. Why are negotiation skills important in all walks of life?

2. What was the final ransom paid to the kidnappers of the politician's aunt?

3. Why is knowing what drives the counterparty important during a negotiation?

4. Why do we need others to listen to our negotiation discussions?

5. Why is "Bending the Reality" important?

6. What role does creating an atmosphere of fairness play in negotiations?

7. How does mirroring help during discussions?

8. What is labeling, and how does it help?

9. What does maintaining intermittent silences during negotiations accomplish?

10. Why is applying the concept of tactical empathy important?

11. Negotiation is nothing but communication with results. Discuss.

12. How do emotions and emotional intelligence assist during a negotiation?

TRIVIA QUESTIONS ABOUT CHRIS VOSS AND TAHL RAZ OF NEVER SPLIT THE DIFFERENCE: NEGOTIATING AS IF YOUR LIFE DEPENDED ON IT

1. What is the name of the company founded by Chris Voss?

2. What is the agency that Chris Voss spent much of his career with?

3. What is the name of the Tahl Raz's New York Times bestseller?

4. Apart from being an author, what else does Tahl Raz do in life?

5. Name some institutions where Chris Voss has taught.

DISCUSSION QUESTIONS OF NEVER SPLIT THE DIFFERENCE: NEGOTIATING AS IF YOUR LIFE DEPENDED ON IT

1. How did the two crisis situations involving the Abu Sayyaf group differ?

2. What are the lessons from the hostage crisis in Rochester, New York, in 1981?

3. How do questions starting with "What" help during negotiations?

4. What are the three types of negotiators, and how should you deal with each of them?

5. How does asking calibrated "How" questions help?

6. How are questions leading to "No" answers better than those leading to "Yes"
answers?

7. How can you spot liars and deal with jerks during discussions?

8. Why is understanding the team members behind the scenes important?

Thank You

I hope you've enjoyed your reading experience.

I and the team at Go BOOKS will always strive to deliver to you the highest-quality summary guides.

So I'd like to thank you for supporting us and reading until the very end.

Before you go, would you mind leaving us a review on Amazon?

It would mean the world to us and support us in creating high-quality guides for you in the future.

Thanks once again, and here's where you can leave a review.

Warmly yours,

The Go BOOKS Team

Made in the USA
Coppell, TX
01 March 2020

16389959R00032